Unlocked & Unleashed: The God Within You

Divine Father Speaks

CHIREYA

Unlocked & Unleashed: The God Within You

Divine Father Speaks

CHIREYA

BOOK 1: CODES OF UNION

CHIREYA

Foxy Creations Worldwide

Unlocked & Unleashed: The God Within You

Divine Father Speaks

Codes of Union Companion Book To:

Codes of Union: Divine Mother Speaks (Coming Soon)

and

Falling In Love with The Beloved Within: Source Speaks (Coming Soon)

ORIGINAL COVER ART BY CHIREYA

CHIREYA.COM

#chireya #arigurudevi

ISBN 978-0-9907498-1-3

"Dear planetary brothers and sisters, if you see the light in these writings, the light is in you. This impeccable timing book will be the light shining on your path to find your own Period of Illumination the ancient ones prophesied. Join the awakened ones and help humanity transcend into a World of Love, Peace and Harmony under the sixth Sun."

~ Don Jose' Munoz, Maya Daykeeper and Guardian of Kame Cimi, 33rd Crystal Skull of Manifestation

"Everything is energy and that's all there is to it. Match the frequency of the reality you want and you cannot help but get that reality. It can be no other way. This is not philosophy. This is physics."

~ Albert Einstein

"God dwells in you, as you, and you don't have to 'do' anything to be God-realized or Self-realized, it is already your true and natural state. Just drop all seeking, turn your attention inward, and sacrifice your mind to the One Self-radiating in the Heart of your very being."

~Ramana Maharshi

"Seek ye first the Kingdom of Heaven,
and all else shall be added unto you…
The Kingdom of Heaven is within you."

~Yeshua, Jesus the Christ

"The kind of seed sown will produce that kind of fruit. Those who do good will reap good results. Those who do evil will reap evil results. If you carefully plant a good seed, You will joyfully gather good fruit."

~Dhammapada

"Whatever precious jewel there is in the heavenly worlds, there is nothing comparable to one who is Awakened."

~The Buddha

"I wish I could show you when you are lonely or in darkness the astonishing light of your own being."

~Hafiz

ACKNOWLEDGMENTS

Nandhiji, Vernon M. Sylvest,
RamaJon, Cherie Mason, Don Jose´ Muñoz,
Tom Bird, Deva Michelle McCune, Michael Perlin,
Ken Rohla, Tamber Bennatt Zawadski, Benjamin Fox,
Zachary Fox, Larry and Tryna Cooper, Stephen Fantl,
Kyra Storojev, Rachel Prince, Brian Dickinson,
J. Christie, George Cruger, Daniel Cruger,
Peter Cruger, all my ancestors and
relatives, countless amazing
friends seen and unseen
who support and
enliven me
in my path
of service
& love.

ALSO BY CHIREYA

Love's Whisperings: Authentic Spiritual Development

with Chireya & The Star Elders

Forthcoming As of This Printing:

Codes of Union Book II
Divine Mother Speaks

Codes of Union Book III
Falling In Love with the Love Within You:
Source Speaks

The Heart of Collaboration:

Co-Creation Through the Unified Field

The Mechanics of Forgiveness

UNCONDITIONAL LOVE IS A TRIP WELL WORTH TAKING

UNCONDITIONAL LOVE IS A TRIP well worth taking. It will work you and cajole you and tattle on you and love you to pieces so you can put yourself back together again in the right order. It will point out all the places where you are NOT unconditionally loving towards yourself and others, and it will caress those sore spots even while scolding you.

The scolding and caressing are One in the most tender love imaginable. It will show you all the places where you've projected your pain onto others, and find a way through the seeming impossible task of assisting you in releasing that resistance and coming to forgive yourself unconditionally for less than ideal creations. It will sit in your lap and slap your face playfully and tickle you and point out the path to liberation from all your worst nightmares. While it's doing that, it may feel scary, horrifying, or even downright humiliating. However, being Unconditional Love, it does this with zero judgment because, YOU ASKED FOR IT. So you can heal. Finally.

Love, Chireya

DEDICATION

TO THE FATHER PRINCIPLE within all life, the seed pattern or "Pater" of Creation Itself, this book is dedicated. The Divine Father within each of us brings wisdom, discernment, and true Self Love through discipline, awareness and comprehension of the Great Law Aback All Things. Divine Father brings the message of Personal Responsibility, and negates the false god's claim of Culpability while helping us do the inner work necessary to truly realize we are at Cause in our lives.

This book is dedicated also to the Divine Mother Principle within all life, the "matter" upon which the seed of Father, the pattern, is imprinted to set life into motion on all levels and in all dimensions.

In equal measure to Father's teaching of self-responsibility and discernment, Mother brings the message of eternal love without conditions and the true comprehension of our Innate Innocence. Together, this Father-Mother Principle births great Compassion for all of life, as we throw off the detritus of the past and claim our True Divine Heritage, The God Within Us.

CONTENTS

FOREWORD BY NANDHIJI

CHIREYA ARIGURU DEVI is an ancient evolved Soul who cares for humanity. Her inspired work as a leader of the community, a visionary, a guide and her other roles, make her life a teaching through example. This Book *Unlocked & Unleashed: The God Within You* holds a potent message with relevant and timely teaching and guidance for humanity. I feel heart wisdom in these words as profound as ancient wisdom, and presented in a way that this wisdom can be used for effective transformation.

Chireya shares the grace of this wisdom with clarity. She writes, "The ordeal of squeezing all that you are into an illusory box was a painstaking process.

No one knew what would happen. But now we know. The experiment is coming to a close, and you the Master Magician, are beginning to awaken to the power that you Are."

Another profound statement in the book, speaks to

the powerful transformative times we are blessed to live in: "The time is now for this Mastery Teaching to be released in your world, and the cosmos watches with baited breath as you offer that Service which will allow you to take your place among the ranks of the Ascended Beings of pure awareness who serve Reality, the One Truth behind all truths."

To leverage the wisdom in *Unlocked & Unleashed: The God Within You* is to awaken to our fullest potential unhindered by limitations of body, mind and karmic patterns.

The profound wisdom that Chireya shares evolves the reader through time tested tools of consciousness used by the yogis of India and realized Masters of all cultures by way of self-inquiry, erasing karma through forgiveness, initiating liberation sequences through codes to work the process of understanding and realization, and other insightful guidance.

This is a book that must be read with reverence to each word, digested and read again as it holds invaluable truth that not only sets us free, but enables us to rise up to our vastness and make definite collective change for humanity as evolved Angelic Beings.

~ Nandhiji

Author, *Mastery of Consciousness- Awaken the Inner Prophet*

Founder, Declaration of Consciousness Movement

INTRODUCTION

THERE IS AN ANCIENT LONGING deep within the heart of every created Being that cannot be quenched by worldly things no matter how many lovers, flavors and adventures we experience.

This longing within is like a cry for HOME though the memory of our true home is distant indeed. We devise ways and means to attempt to fill this void, and eventually through lifetime after lifetime of experience, we realize the phenomenal world can only satisfy us so much. While we can embrace the worldly joy of people, places and things, there is nothing that will satisfy this longing once and for all, other than the recognition and realization that Source, or God is within us, and that this Source is pure love.

The process of unleashing and unlocking the God Within is called Self-Realization, Enlightenment, Awakening, and other things across all cultures.

Great masters and yogis across all time have

experienced the full realization of this God Within and have brought Messages to the many seeking respite and real knowledge.

For those who are able to simply drop into the Self Within, this book may not be necessary, as there is nothing else to attain or know. For those who are still on the path seeking clarification and comprehension of how and why existence might have come into being, how pain and suffering might have transpired, and how to make one's way out of this pain and suffering back to the bliss of primordial self-realization, this book is offered as a loving and compassionate tool of this comprehension.

The messages of the primordial masculine aspect of First Cause (God, Source, Principle), called Divine Father or simply Father in this book, takes us on a cosmic journey from the beginning of Creation into a comprehension of the Action of the Law and Compounded Momentum, helping catalyze our consciousness towards Self-Responsibility as Beings of God and Co-creators. In the next book of the Codes of Union Series, we will hear from Divine Mother.

Divine Father also explains in this tome, how and why the Grand Experiment was begun by Source Beings flung into outer space in a multi-dimensional holographic adventure of phenomenal creation, venturing into innumerable star systems, galaxies and universes for the purpose of experience and self-reflection.

Divine Father lovingly guides us into the openness to begin to remember that we are ONE with Him, and therefore with all of Life, just as we are ONE with Divine Mother and Source Itself.

Through comprehension of this Oneness combined with personal discipline, discernment of an internal nature, and awareness, we can recalibrate ourselves back to union with the Spark of Spirit within. This "Spark" is the true self—that "little piece of God" that willingly flung itself into the Grand Experiment we call "life."

A perspective is shared here on a question that many have pondered over the eons: How and why was the "dark side" created? Could it be that "we" the adventurers through space time unknowingly and innocently created it ourselves, through our lack of awareness of the Action of the Law and our subsequent projection onto the so called "other"? If this is true, then all forgiveness is Self-Forgiveness, and the healing of a dismantled, distorted world can take place within each of us with the comprehension of total safety and unconditional love.

"We Are All Source," says Father. "We are ONE. There is no Other." All the great wisdom sages reflect this teaching, through their Direct Experience. Father lets us know that the Stage is Set, for a Grand Awakening on this planet, the Final Act of the Great Play which is this multi-versal, multi-dimensional Experiment in Co-creation.

Willingly and one by one, through the power of our God Given free will, we each come to a place in life where the prerogative is to look within for God.

Following in the footsteps of great Masters such as Yeshua-Jesus, Buddha, Mohammed, and sages such as Ramana Maharshi, Yogananda and countless other reflections of this ONE within, we have finally suffered enough. We raise the white flag and surrender to the longing for this Grand Reunion. Many are the Pathways HOME to God. We are as individuated reflections, rays beaming forth from this Great Cosmic Pool of All That Is. Bathe in the waters of this message, and soothe your soul with Divine Comprehension. And then, go forth and do the Mighty Work of sitting in the stillness to realize through wisdom, compassion and grace this Divine God Within You.

Your Presence on the planet with this intention, however small or large it may be right now, is catalyzing consciousness on a global scale. It is YOUR mercy, and YOUR grace, YOUR light, and YOUR love that is cascading through you to a world in need, a world that has grown weary of endless cycles of suffering.

I celebrate you in your awakening and unfoldment in the Light of Truth of the God Within You, and I give thanks for your Presence on this little sphere, in service to an awakening humanity. May mercy and grace follow you, all the days of your life.

~Chireya

WHEN CREATION WAS NEW: YOUR DESIRE TO EXPLORE

This is Father speaking.

REMEMBER A TIME WHEN creation was new. Brave sovereigns emerged from Source for an intergalactic adventure like none before.

You were young.

Your hopes for the dance of this universal experience were many, while the unknowns were enticing to the curious parts of you.

Heaven's gate opened wide and you ushered forth in all your glory, together as One yet also as Many. At that time within the cycle, it was not known how things would play out. In fact, that was the point! Adventure was afoot and you were all about it.

Time passes and you grow. Much like the orange tree, the fruit of your experience ripens with each galactic episode. New timelines in the array of probability fields displayed before you are ushered in, and in between lifetimes, you chose your destiny.

There is no right or wrong, only growth, clarity and awareness. As Ensouled Spirit, God in a body, you gain wisdom, knowledge and skill, and embark upon a journey which brings you untold numbers of experiences created right out of the fabric of the universe.

Who are you?

How did you get here?

Where are you going?

These are the questions you are continually aligning with, consciously or unconsciously, in each now moment of this ongoing creation. As a Source Streaming Human Angel, now clothed with flesh and awakening to the Truth of you, you are donned with glory as you remember the God Within You, though the garment of the created mind called SOUL might feel heavy from layers of compounded momentum generated through eons of time and experience. But wait — you are not the mind, you are pure Spirit! And as Spirit you have traveled far and journeyed long to get to this place of awakening after drifting into a long slumber.

The trials and tribulations of this lifetime are many, yet somehow, somewhere inside you is that unquenchable Spark of life, of light, from which you came and to which you will one day return — but not yet, because your hunger for experience is not yet satisfied! You hunger also for the perspective that will set you free from all that is illusion.

As the Master Magician, you have set a trap for yourself so convincing, that you do not yet recall that it was by your own intent, power, and will that the trap was set to begin with.

How would you, an unlimited being, be able to have an experience of limitation without a very convincing net?

The ordeal of squeezing all that you are into an illusory box was a painstaking process. No one knew what would happen. But now we know. The experiment is coming to a close, and you the Master Magician, are beginning to awaken to the power that you Are. The stakes seem high, as all that has been gathered in torrents of momentous events on this planet is coming to a head. The stage is set for your Grand Awakening, the Grand Illumination. It is a tender and precious time, yet rife with many complexities.

Why are things the way they are?

Why have you had painful and treacherous

experiences in this life on earth?

Why is there so much love and so

much hate simultaneously?

Why does it appear so difficult to overcome the energetics

of the past—with a momentum like boulders

careening down a hill?

All these questions and more, we will address in this book. You will find solace and comfort here, along with the kick in the arse you need to move beyond the illusory self-imposed confines of a creator gone mad.

This Madness that led to the decision you made to embark upon this journey has the spirit of True Love within it. Self-responsibility is the Name of the Game of awakening, as the Love that you Are embraces the Truth of You. Never has there been a grander, more phenomenal experience in all of creation. The multi-versal awareness of God Beings everywhere are at the edge of their cosmic seats to see what happens next!

A FOUNDATION OF TRUTH: CODES OF LIBERATION

THE ROCK SOLID TRUTH at the foundation of this universal experiment is unwavering. It is completely dependable. It had to be get you where you are, and where you're going. This basic platform of existence says, "That which goes around, comes around."

It had to be dependable if you were to jettison yourself out into the unknown in proportions never before seen in all creation. The Law is this foundation. The Law is your rope; the Law is your rock. You are as firmly tethered to this rope as the sun is to the Galactic core, and more.

The Law can defy gravity, but gravity cannot defy The Law. Your reliance upon it can be whole and complete, as you make your way back to the Captain's Seat of the Ship of your Life. Never before in human history has there been such an upswelling of desire for this Truth.

Return to the foundation of the Law and peel away the layers of falsehood and disguise so you can be free.

So what is this Law? And how can it be leveraged to get yourself and yourselves out of the tangled mess resulting from eons of compounded momentum that accrued "while you weren't watching?" If you are Source, and you are at your core, then it is logical to assume you have been equipped with all the attributes of this One Source.

And what might those be? The logos – *the word* – ushers from your lips as from the lips of God, your primordial parent, your primordial Self. This logos or logoi, acts upon the substance as the sperm unto an ovum. The seed is planted, the energy of creation is summoned, and something new is born. This is the birds and bees story of creation and you have a part in it. These are the facts of life. It is very basic, and yet everything in creation is based upon it. Thus it is foundational.

Without comprehending this foundation, it is impossible for you to know who you are and how you got here. Thus the time it takes to fully ground yourself in this principle is well worth it. *Principle: that which is primary, that which comes first.* This principle is firm, like the firmament of heaven above. Unshakeable, Unmovable. Never Changing, Always Present. Dependable. Like a Good Father. A Shepard, a Steward—there for you, to guide you, always. That is why the Law is Lord. Respect is due.

As souls progress in evolution towards what we might call spiritual maturity, different Key Codes begin to be unlocked within the being, to set the stage for the next phase of growth.

These Key Codes are triggered by the cascading energies of a major sequence of events, which trigger graduation to the next level like grades in a classroom.

When the soul is ready, the next code required for its development automatically unlocks. These codes were designed long ago by . . . guess who? You got it: You.

You knew when you flung yourselves out here into creation, that this guidance system would become necessary for you to calibrate to the perfectly timed Grand Awakening, assisting you in your return HOME, to share the wisdom and inspiration you have received on your long journey, and to rest.

The codes of creation once accessed, are forever life changing for the being unlocking them. It is now a time of Master Key Codes unlocking whole new sets of codes ushering in a completely different platform from the one upon which you stand now. You've been preparing for this change for a very long time, in human terms. Yet it is as the blink of an eye, from the cosmic perspective.

Many are the sojourns and lonely nights as the soul seeks reunion with its Source. Many are the dramas played out, as the unquestioning thirst for a return to love grows stronger with each lifetime. Eventually nothing else will do, but reunion with the Self, God within.

God Within is ever present, all knowing and all powerful, behind the curtain of consciousness. Heartbreaks, successes, trials and tribulations; husbands and wives; children, careers, fame and fortune—all these are like flickers on a movie screen compared to the Life that resides within you.

Dissatisfaction ensues, after a lifetime upon lifetime, the worldly cup has not quenched this thirst to know and love your Self as One with all. This is when the soul begins to question and seek, and the seeker shall find.

Because of the nature of the Law and the unceasing orchestra of compounded momentum, the soul has many layers to peel away before it can lay naked to The Truth.

This process can feel arduous, at times full of mystery, and at others, full of glory. The shadow play underway in the living dream of a world with characters playing their roles seems so real—but is it? This depends on how you define reality. The Supreme Reality is beyond the shadow play, and the play could not exist without the stage which is the Source behind all phenomena.

It is simple really, once a being truly wishes to comprehend the nature of reality and the pre-existant Self. This necessitates a desire to move beyond what we might lovingly call, the playthings of a childish mind. In the process, it may feel difficult to directly experience the fullness of Divine Realization. This "supreme" desire will shapeshift into and masquerade temporarily as a desire to find Love outside of the Self, in others or the world. The world's forms are fleeting, and it may feel like there is nothing to hold onto. This can cause a feeling of panic or stress in this "in between zone." Eventually a being will learn to let go of clinging and float in the Sea of Love without "needing to know" or hold onto phenomena to replace the sense of security and peace which will eventually arise with realization.

And this "Truth" can indeed be experienced and remembered from within the phenomenal world. A different approach is required to experience this, as fleeting form cannot be held onto to quench an eternal thirst. One must rest in the background energy, in the Truth of our Pre-existent Oneness. The phenomenal world of form which is the dance of Maya changes on purpose. It is part of the design.

Resting in the Oneness feels like "home" and "peace." It is not a static peace, but a dynamic flow state beyond the ordinary "mind." A different part of the brain becomes dominant, and beings connect with this Unity Consciousness while experiencing life in a body. Duality and the "fight or flight mode" collapses, allowing us to deeply rest in our experience of ultimate connection with All That Is, at One with it, even while we experience ourselves as individuated beings. From this place of rest, peace and oneness, we have access to the energy that creates worlds, this time, consciously. There is no grasping, clinging or neediness present in this state of mind. All things become possible, and nothing is required to feel complete. This is attainable by all.

WELCOME HOME

WELCOME HOME to the Truth of You. To glimpse this Truth is to light a fire within the soul so strong that there is nothing in creation which can keep this fire from becoming an Inferno. This Spiritual Fire is the cleansing fire which purifies the soul from the detritus of the accumulated compounded experience. This detritus or "energetic debris" is the sticky, waxy residue that crescendos outward in consciousness and imprints its own pattern onto form. Think of it like a slide in a slide projector. The light of Source *must* project the information in the slide onto the screen of our reality. Thus, the material in our conscious and unconscious databanks outpicture into our reality, causing the continual repetition of the very pattern in the slide. When beings do not know the mechanism behind this cascade of experience into reality, this can cause confusion as well as cyclical repetition of patterns desired or undesired.

The being experiencing the repetition, if asleep,

spiritually speaking, can become quite distressed in its forgetfulness.

Why me?

Where did I go wrong?

What's wrong with me?

And now we can see how the Action of the Law works even when we are not aware of it. This awareness itself is that mercy and grace which will recalibrate the soul to its own knowing of Itself.

Painful and traumatic lifetimes have left their scars, and beyond forgetfulness, the healing begins in earnest once this Inferno within has been ignited. This is because the tempering of the sword has taken place, and the being is now ready to take up the Sword of Personal Responsibility.

Without claiming responsibility for that which has transpired, it is not possible to fully embrace these teachings and this Law. And simultaneously without comprehending the nature of compounding momentum through multitudes of time, it is not possible for the idea of the Law to make sense.

A typical human being comes into this earthly plane with few to no memories of "the before times"—past lives and multi-dimensional experience, and little to no conscious access to the records of the ancestors. Because of this forgetfulness, the world seems utterly illogical. There appears to be a lack of order where unfairness and unkindness run rampant without meaning. Until we can fully comprehend the nature of the Law, our multi-dimensional existence, and compounded momentum, we cannot see our role in the making of All That Is. To embrace the Truth of the mechanism of how life works is to set ourselves free.

For example, let's look at the life of a typical human being. This person has a body, mind, emotions, and a soul. This person is a Spirit—a spark of the eternal One. This being has had many lifetimes, in which he or she has accrued many experiences. These experiences get our attention and are therefore are causative to further thoughts, words, feelings and actions. This causes what we call compounded momentum of particular patterns of behavior, thought and experience through time and space. The beings' ancestors have also accumulated much such experience and momentum, and the residue of all this resides as tendencies of thought, emotions and feelings which give rise to further actions, more deeply engraining the pattern into the body of the being.

The nature of the choices made in any life stream and the subsequent actions that arise as a result, leads to more experiences with the same pattern indelibly imbedded within them as imprints, and so forth, ad infinitum. The entire lineage is affected by the tendencies of thought, word and action sustained or initiated by a lineage member in the present. Those who are more spiritually advanced may be less affected, yet still may be suffering from problems the source of which may seem elusive. The root of the problem is potentially from ancestral compounded momentum.

Pretty soon in cosmic terms, it is as if a huge ball of

debris is accumulated and over time, hardens into stone. This stone topples by its own weight gathering moss as it careens the being into what we call "fate." This is because the ball acts as a magnet, buried deep in the unconscious of the being. This magnet-like ball is inherently programmed to attract more of all the things that are like the pattern, into the life stream.

As the nature of the Law is Lord and rules all, there is no stopping the ball. It must be dismantled, which also means, it must be seen as the illusion it is, albeit at this point, it has become an entirely convincing illusion. The "reality" of the beliefs, experiences and structures experienced have solidified.

When the structures are so entirely perceived as real, to the point where a suffering being would not be able to escape the delusional trap of its own making without help, this dismantling occurs by grace. Waving the White Flag of Surrender, a soul declares truce with Life Itself and embarks upon a self-correcting course. The being will encounter new experiences which will assist him or her in utilizing his or her own God-given gifts of creation to recalibrate to the Truth of Itself as Cause. Equipped with this knowledge, the being becomes wise enough to employ its own God Given heritage of intent, focus, deletion and the inherent power of Source, to course-correct and clear things up.

This recursive, self-correcting process dismantles the energetics of the past by bringing in the fresh perspective of Self as God. If you are the God of your Life, then certainly you can decide and cut away all that is not desired. The awareness of oneness with Source or God is not the same as what is known as spiritual ego or megalomania. In spiritual ego or megalomania, the "mind" of the personality believes *it* is God, whereas it is only a teensy aspect of All That Is and does not have access to the full quotient of Love-Light of the Absolute Harmonic Universe. The spiritually egoic being may suffer from delusions of grandeur or identify with Gods or Goddesses, Archangels or Demons from history. There are many influences that can cause this. The main point to take away, is that the awakened being realizes its Oneness with All That Is from a place of humility and wonder, self respect and respect for others, who are necessarily, also At One with this selfsame Source. And whether they realize it or not, the awakened one has begun to comprehend this, birthing great compassion and love for all.

As the awakening game continues, self-reflective positive action leads to personal growth and worldly results. Now, the momentum begins compounding in the other direction, and as always, the Law is there to back everyone up. The Law has never abandoned anyone, though it may have felt as though it did. Leveraging the Godly Powers of thoughts, words, feelings and deeds, the momentum builds in the direction of loving, desired fruits.

Knowing the True Self more and more each day, the prerogative of the awakening being is to design life intentionally. Yet and still, the momentum of the culture cascades into collective experience, and there are some trains no one can stop—trains that are already in fierce motion towards a destination patterned by the accumulated karmas of the past.

Knowing this, we can breathe deep compassion into our hearts as we witness a young humanity unknowingly driving itself into a ditch. You the awakening ones are here as elder souls now, to soften the blow with your loving thoughts, words, actions and deeds—knowingly this time, from the depths of true love in your being. Yet you find yourself in a soup of seeming unstoppable madness, among people who no more think they are God then they think the sun is a raisin. And on certain days, the milieu makes it difficult to remember the Law yourself, and you seem to slip. Oh, what to do?

The truth of our Original Unity lends clues to this divine perplexity. The Truth that "there is only one of us here" lends a hand. If this is true, and it is, this is one step towards realizing that what we do for ourselves, affects the All.

Compassion is birthed through comprehension. In a world where forgetfulness has reigned for so long, compassion is truly in order. The birth of Compassion is the healing balm that stokes the spark into an absolute Inferno of Spiritual Love-Wisdom, assisting us in finally accessing true self love, which is the same as love of all.

This Light and Love of Spirit always has been and

always will be within, quietly awaiting this moment of reckoning.

THE EVER PRESENT NOW: INFINITY LOOPS, ETERNITY IS

SUPPLIED WITH THIS KNOWLEDGE, it becomes possible to peek through the masks of the simplest of souls who have all but forgotten Spirit is real. Peeking through these masks, you can now see God within their eyes too. Truth reveals that ALL are God, not just you or the enlightened masters of old—and logic dictates it is so if we accept the foundational wisdom aback these words.

Equipped with this insight, it becomes easier to forgive others for we now understand how they got where *they* are in life, too.

Once we fully and TRULY forgive ourselves, it becomes impossible to hold others in anything other than unconditional love. This is a natural process of spiritual maturation backed by scientific principle and the Action of the Law.

The God of our Being is not a God of wrath but a God of Love. "Mercy and grace shall follow you all the days of your life." It is but we who must forgive ourselves, as the Source Creator of our being has never held judgments of any kind against us.

By setting forth the Law as Lord, the Supreme Creator gave us a tether. This guiding line also acts as a warning, like the stroke of a whip that is self-activated and self-perpetuated by each being through the Action of the Law Itself in any circumstance.

Do you see the beauty of it now? The creator is not whipping us; we who embarked on this journey with this great Law behind us originally and willingly are whipping ourselves. We decided we needed to have this check and balance if we were to go forth into a Free Will Experiment.

We both suffer and benefit from the action of this Law accordingly, based on the choices we make with our own God-given free will. Nothing could be more beautiful and self-contained. We are the Cause of our own happiness, we are the Cause of our own suffering. At one with the Cause of all causes, we can rejoice as we realize the absolute perfection of this Divine Plan.

Recognizing ourselves now in the eyes of each being we encounter, Mercy is truly ours. And the agreement was, each one shall have that free will to choose, always. Respect and honor is due. The choice of each one is the gift given by the Prime Creator at the beginning of this Grand Experiment. God or Source is the very essence of each being, and this Source has bestowed freedom unto Itself for the purpose of self exploration. Embodying as All That Is, this Source has had eons of experience and is learning and integrating from the pleasant and the unpleasant.

From this perspective, the folly of judgment becomes clear. We would be judging our very own self in the person of another, and causing the boomerang effect of the Law to return to us in the form of "being judged." We would feel the feeling of this judgment and eventually experience all repercussions from that thought form set into motion. This letting go of judgment does not mean we let go of discernment. We simply learn to utilize the dynamic forces at play consciously, to now create a counter intention for ourselves and our loved ones that balances out the playing field and sets us to steering the ship of our own lives in the direction of our choosing.

The one seemingly in need of our judgment is our very own Self having an experience of Its own making. Who are we to judge or say this being we are witnessing ought to have done it differently? This is a bitter pill to swallow, as this means "allowing" suffering as well as joy. It is difficult to watch others suffer at their own hands, yet we can extend our love to all unconditionally, like light from the rays of the sun, to lend comfort where comfort is needed.

Perhaps the very essence of that light you shine is the balm needed to ripen this soul into a desire to change. And, how can we know whether or not the seemingly painful experience of this "other" playing out before our eyes, is the perfect scenario for tempering the sword of that being to ripen them into awakening?

Resting in awe of the Divine Plan, all there is to do is Love unconditionally. Realizing that All That Is As It Is

Because It *Is*, we learn to act with discernment, make good choices for ourselves, and yet, withhold our love from no one. Through this process, we become wise enough to embrace and now fully understand the tenet, "Judge not lest ye be judged."

MISCREANTS AND VAGRANTS ON THE PATH TO ENLIGHTENMENT

WE ENCOUNTER FROM TIME TO TIME some souls who seem so crystallized towards the darkness that it appears there is no hope for them. In fact, many such blatant miscreants adorn the world stage with worldly power garnered through another usage of the Law.

Could it be true we are to forgive even them? How could it be possible that they and we are One? Their behavior seems so foreign to the Love we seek to restore to the world and ourselves.

However, if looked upon correctly, in fact they can become our greatest teachers. There is no love lost on the human plane between perpetrators and their victims. And yet to have been able to garner power over others and still navigate the Law consciously, some of these perpetrators have learned to leverage the Law in a very particular way. Through understanding the principles of free will and compounded momentum, such beings carefully orchestrate events that cause the operation of the Law to take place upon the consciousness of their subjects, to the ends of their own choosing. This is in congruence with the Law of Free Will, though it is of course a negative usage of the Law and ends up having vast karmic consequences for all who partake. If this tactic is to work, it is ideal that the subjects forget the Truth of Who they are. If someone does not know the God power within them, it is much easier to deceive them.

The dispensation to assist beings who have been caught as subjects in such a web of trickery comes from the core of Source itself, to rectify situations and liberate beings who would otherwise innocently be caught in endless cycles of Looping.

This Looping Mechanism comes from the very Law of which we speak. The Law Itself can be utilized to create great beauty, harmony and love upon a planetary sphere, or it can be turned against beings without their knowledge of it to force outcomes that are desired by the designers of the trickery.

The subjects of this dark ploy get caught into endless cycles of death and rebirth, like slaves to a self-created prison, albeit they're not aware of the prison, the prison guards or the Law that binds them.

To further clarify the point, some of those who wish to consciously align with the dark, which is nothing more than a path of deceit and power mongering, have also determined how to work within the confines of the base platform of reality, the Law and Free Will.

If they are aware of the Law and wish to manipulate others, these perpetrators have discovered ways to orchestrate situations to cause their victims to activate the power of God within in directions of *their* choosing, secretly.

This causative impulse of injected thought forms and ideas acts upon the Law like any other self-begotten impulse, and people who have been imprinted get caught in a web of delusion and lies. The purposeful mass withholding of the knowledge of God within is the key factor in being able to manipulate others into creations not of their conscious choosing.

This Actionable, Eternal Law governs those who are hell bent on dark acts as well as those of the light, as this Law is the Foundational Principle of this particular cosmic experience in which we find ourselves.

Thus it is important to realize that the key factor in liberation from this manipulation is personal responsibility, the sanction of God the Father. Personal responsibility is the Sword of Truth of God the Father.

The masculine energy of discernment, definition and decision allows us to see clearly and cut away anything we have created or attracted that is not beneficial. It is the Protector aspect of creation. As such it carries a template of self-preservation which is also self-responsibility.

As a God Being, your mechanism of thought, word, feelings and imagination sends forth a vibratory frequency that creates a pattern-match to similar things. Like attracts like. Once conscious of this, your power is unstoppable to redirect things in your own favor and subdue the tempest of subconscious imprints whether self-generated or perpetrated on you by a seeming "other."

Without understanding this, it is not possible to fully free oneself from the patterns of karma or the trickery of miscreants who desire control. Embracing total self-responsibility, you become able to dismantle the false or faulty manifestations of past egoic creations. Ego means "of the mind" which is apparently (but not actually) separated from Source.

It is not possible to actually be separated from Source, because Source is All There Is.

Everything that ever has been made, has been made from Source Energy and Source Substance. That means by definition, that even those beings we deem "dark" have come from Source Energy originally, however preposterous that may seem from the limited human point of view.

The mantle of fear comes from this false mind and has no foundation in truth. Fear makes the idea of separation real, and makes the "other" an enemy. Truth knows that you and I are One. Truth knows that life is eternal, and so are you. Truth embraces reality in its original form, that of Oneness, Unity, and Wholeness.

This wholeness and Truth cannot be held apart from any aspect of creation, if it is in fact Truth. That means even these miscreants of torment and vagrants of delusion are, in fact, other ones of ourselves, aspects of a Creator gone mad, kind of like illusory projections of the One which is, all of us.

But practically speaking, how does one dismantle the subconscious thought forms secretly implanted by these seemingly external unsavory controllers?

First and foremost, take responsibility for the Self. Remember, there is no Other. "They" are "You" in another form, and you are "Creator."

You are the First Cause of your reality, and therefore even though your awareness is only beginning to peek through the curtain of lies, you indeed do have Dominion over all aspects of your creation, when you choose to become aware and leverage this.

Thus you can command that all patterns, forces, energetics, hexes, curses, ideas, belief systems, thought forms, pictures, structures and anything else created to intentionally harm or derail you from the truth be demolished once and for all from your subconscious mind and your conscious mind, in depth and permanently, on all levels in all layers, in all times, spaces and dimensions, in all hidden layers, and in all concepts of time.

Call upon the Prime Creator within you, the Source of All Sources, Being of All Beings, Love of All Loves, Essence of All Essences, and "ask" that these things be cleared from your body, mind, soul, emotions and spirit; in your ancestral lineages forward and backward in time; and in all your past, future and parallel lives, as well as in this life.

Call upon forgiveness for all beings everywhere who have anything to do with this undesired manifestation. Most of all, forgive your very own Self, for if you are in fact at One with the Prime Cause, then in some mysterious, forgotten way, *you* set all of this in motion to begin with. THIS is radical self-love; this is radical self-responsibility. And this is the absolute MAGIC behind seeming miracles.

In this way, the subconscious pathways finally clear

once and for all, and can now open up and become able to receive the new positive, useful, desired imprints you choose from your own conscious awareness and true Self Love.

It is the "asking" which is the key. The Commander General of Your Own Life, you hold the key. You just have to remember this is so, and relinquish the energetics and ideas of being subordinate to anyone or anything.

In Your Realm you are Sovereign. It has always been this way, and will always be, unless you choose of your own free will to create it differently, and subject yourself to others. This subjection can take place simply by being born into a planetary sphere in which these conditions already exist. By showing up, you tacitly permit this subjection, until you don't.

If it is true that these things have been perpetrated on humanity to perpetuate a game of control and power, and that this game is being played consciously by "the few" and unconsciously participated in by "the many," then we can see that the floodgates of compassion can now open even more, as we become aware of what has transpired, and the deep suffering that has been experienced as a result.

It is this compassion which breeds mercy and grace to assist beings in untangling these knots. It is a gift of the Self to the self. If Self is all there is, then this selfsame one IS these perpetrators and these victims. Realizing what It has done, mercy is extended unto It's very own self in the form of these ones so subjected. It is after all a Free Will Universe, and in that free will experiment, no limitations were placed on beings, but the Law was put there to ensure an immutable check and balance system through which beings eventually learn.

Many are the factors which accrue to energize a being's subconscious and conscious mind with patterns and vibrations that have led to the current experience.

Most of these factors are hidden to modern man and woman, thus, the "why" of their lives remains a mystery. This phenomenon causes much grief and confusion when full comprehension is not present. When we begin to see that unwholesome intentional imprints from the present and past have added unto the compounded momentum already in play, it is easy to comprehend that though we are all Creators, we did not necessarily consciously "intend" for things to turn out as the suffering we've experienced. We become aware of the deeper complexities as we realize the impact of this momentum on both soul and past life levels, combined with the cultural conditioning of the milieu in which beings live.

This is where the codes of Divine Mother come into play: claim your Divine Innocence, and love yourself unconditionally. Embrace all of it, including the tears, the rage, the grief and the fear. Love these emotions into submission to the Truth that Love never left us at all.

We can further understand the teaching of the Great Master Yeshua, also known as Jesus Christ: "Forgive them Father, for they know not what they do." It is this Mercy and Grace of the Divine Mother's Love and remembrance of your Intrinsic Innocence, coupled with the Sword of Truth and the teachings of Self Responsibility herein set forth, which will ultimately enable you to set yourself free.

As you long ago set out upon your journey into the

Cosmos from that Original Impulse of Source, you placed this Truth into a Secret Place in your bosom never to be destroyed. This is your Tether and your Rope, connecting you eternally back to the Primordial Reality. You can leverage the power of it, to rebalance the playing field and come to clarity. Even the seeming lowliest creature has this Divine Source connection within. It is the foundation of all created beings. As above, so below. You are the God from which you came.

And yet in this manifest form, your image made in the likeness of your Creator is like unto a reflection in a pool of water. The you that you think you are, the constructed you, is made up of mind stuff and soul experience, and is not the real You. "It" has a consciousness of its own which is the driver of your human experience and desires, until the spiritual restlessness within causes you to seek out and know this deeper self within your bosom.

Your timing is perfect and you are on the right path, as you recalibrate your soul to be able to be become aware of this original Truth. To embrace the Shadow Self, is to realize you created it through unconsciousness. If you are God, then you are All. And now the moment is dawning when you can finally comprehend, why and how all that is came to be.

ESSENCE AND FORM

PRIMORDIAL ESSENCE OOZES OUT into Creation as the stuff that enlivens it. Essence gets particularized by the Action of the Law upon it, through the seed imprint of your very own words, thoughts, feelings and deeds. The vibratory nature of reality reflects into existence an exact picture, an outpicturing, of what you as Creator *say* it will be. The Logos-Logoi or "Word" IN you acts UPON the Law to form matter into being. This is the way it always has been and the way it always will be in this multi-versal, multi-dimensional experience.

Through eons of time and compounded momentum, many great structures have been built, and great beings have designed entire planetary systems as if from thin air. From the grand scale architects of entire solar systems and galaxies to the Universal Oversoul to the ordinary human being, creation works the same way.

Founded upon the selfsame principles of the Law,

this creative process has to do with the seed pattern of the father, "pater," becoming imprinted upon the substance of "matter," the mother. Our clue to this is found in everyday life when we begin to witness the Law in action through application of deliberate intent. In other words, as our deliberately intended creations come into manifestation, we become witness to the mechanism by which creation works. This direct experience is the only way to truly *know* the fact of this.

And because of the phenomenon of compounded momentum over time, it sometimes takes some doing to course correct and direct attention along the lines of your actual current desires. Rivulets of consciousness and tendencies of thought etch themselves into your soul and even your brain, making it easier to take the path well-traveled. Diligence is required to make a change that eventually washes away these stream beds of the brain, forming new pathways from your new habits of thought.

This is where practice makes perfect, and one should not give up just because of a temporary seeming delay in results. But one should prove to oneself with small steps that the Law is in operation, and thereby gain confidence in the Law. That confidence adds to the momentum to strengthen us in asserting our will in subsequent intentions we choose to manifest. As we consciously connect with Source Within before creating, our will and the Will of the Prime Creator become One, ensuring the outcome will be aligned with our greatest good and the greatest good of all.

The proof is in the pudding as they say. But why does the pudding sometimes seem to go sour? This is because the Action of the Law over time and through space and dimension which is causative to your experience, is not obvious to you. It remains cloaked by your somnambulance to the truth of you.

The Action of the Law does not cease from one lifetime to the next, or one moment to the next, nor does it spare those who are unaware of its mechanism.

It could not be Law if it were bendable or changeable. That's why and how many countless beings have gotten caught in a co-creational web of their own making.

As created beings you have chosen to BE. Desires and attachments created by your very own thoughts, words and deeds can become a blessing or a curse. The only way a curse from another being can affect you is if it finds a place to reside within your conscious or subconscious mind.

In light of this, it becomes apparent why the saying goes, "See no evil, hear no evil, speak no evil." This is not a Pollyanna-ish or crude remark to keep people in line, but a magical tenet to instruct you on how to conduct yourself such that the Action of the Law shall go in your favor. The consistent application of these principles over time with what has been called "faith" will wash away remnants of old imprints from various timelines and levels of life.

Faith here is used to describe that process of accepting something as true before we know it as Truth, for the purpose of entraining ourselves to the eventual full realization of that Truth. Faith then becomes knowledge as the consistent application of the Law takes hold and takes root in the subconscious mind, finally superseding less than desired leftovers from untold eons of undesirable compounded momentum. In this way and in your Wisdom, you become aware that there is a juncture—a portalway or gateway "between the worlds"—wherein the old energetics may still be playing themselves out, even as the new energetics are being built from your new intentions and thoughts.

Therefore, in leveraging your intelligence and Divine Logic, you will "be the bridge" for yourself and others, remembering to "give up the old for the new" and become thankful for every circumstance and feeling that arises, as you now KNOW that these old energetics are arising for final completion.

If in your folly you were to react against these undesired occurrences and judge them, yourself or others, you would be unintentionally and unconsciously setting the Law into motion ONCE AGAIN, birthing new energetics of the same kind. That is why the Law of Forgiveness is KING in the recalibration to the Truth of You. Give up the Old for the New. Be done with these remnants. Turn the other cheek of your grasping mind to look only upon Truth which will set you free.

The information, knowledge and power are here, yet the milieu in which you find yourself on this planet at this time does not embrace the truth fully as of yet. People have been trained to entertain thoughts of failure, disease and death. Parents and their forebears have gotten caught up in a legacy which gets translated into the minds of the children by nature of the Law.

And so the looping continues to compound and grow in myriad ways until we have a dynamic and fascinating cultural creation which we call reality. Now imagine that this circumstance has not originated on this planet alone. The human genome and created beings have existed on many planes and planets in many dimensions for unthinkable eons of time. This is how the vast orchestrations of galactic councils and earthly empires, crafts and professions, technology and even the design of creatures and plants, has become so painstakingly intricate. There is much time displayed here, in the details of the ordinary life. Because human beings have forgotten the legacy from which they came, they look out to the world in awe, wondering how it all came to be. It is a mytho-poetic moment when one wonders at the cause of it all, and taps into that mystery which is in fact the Truth of themselves.

The appearance of this seeming complexity may be a temporary obstacle to clearly seeing the pathway HOME to The Truth of You as God. As a created being looking out onto the absolute enormity of the creation in which you find yourself, it is very easy to feel small and insignificant, powerless and unimportant, in the grand scheme of things. Yet contrary to popular belief, you are the Center of your Universe. The Original Singularity is intrinsically connected to the Singularity within you. Humility is in order even while self respect is due.

Fear may arise upon feeling oneself in the midst of this enormous complexity, and may cause a desire for stability—a firm platform upon which to stand within all this vast intricacy and seeming chaos.

The truth is this Firm Platform always is, was and has been. It is called The Law. But if the Law is forgotten, as it has been in many civilizations, the tendency is to look outwards into the world in a vain attempt to find or create this stability in attachment, control and potentially even manipulation of others. Feeling cut off from the Source of Life Within, a being unaware of its true identity and operating from a limited perspective, may feel the need to take matters into its own hands. Fear emerges as a nefarious companion to the desire to control things.

This desire for control is but a childish mimic of a Higher Principle, which is the Truth that each being *is* responsible for co-creating their reality from within, and *can* learn/remember how to do so through conscious mastery of the Action of the Law.

If understood properly, "control" becomes "self-mastery of thought and feeling." Since the mechanism of creation never stops, the desire for control over the outside world and others is fear-based thinking which necessarily imprints the fabric of creation, and once in motion, more societal constructs, systems and things are built from this faulty platform.

All who witness this seemingly solid new reality based on fear, become imprinted with its essence and may begin to believe there is truth within it. Eons of time may pass, with these false creations built on the lie, eventually becoming vast civilizations with complex rules and regulations, beliefs and preferences.

There is great compassion here, as now it is clear to see that these familiar constructs of the mind which have taken shape in the world around us, may never have been built on a firm foundation of Truth at all. But we have become attached to them, and cling to them like a child to a favorite blanket.

Entire civilizations have been built this way, and the Law and rules of these civilizations have become a false Lord, governing people in place of the truth of the Source Within. Stringency in managing the execution of these false god laws becomes something tenaciously held to, for the purpose of feeling safe and secure. This erroneous sense of safety and security by clinging to "the rules" is the offspring of the original fear-thinking that had been set in motion.

And then one day or one lifetime amidst all this compounding creation and fear based, rule based unconscious reality creation, a being begins to awaken.

This sleeping giant stirs and looks out upon the creation and begins to question it.

How in the world did we get here?

Who are we, really?

Is all this chaos and stress really necessary?

And where are we going? Where do we WANT to go?

The inner impulse of this awakening Divine Being has become startled by the frequencies of the seeming fate it feels ensuing. The psychic-aware nature of a being can feel/see impending energies, and the more aware a being becomes of the Source within, the more these "superpowers" activate.

This awakening being feels the impulses that are tugging at the life stream as repercussions of that which had been formerly set into motion. This is but the awareness of the Law in action, the same mechanism used by psychics to detect what might happen next. Your cosmic insight as the Creator allows you to feel frequency, and to have a sense of impending manifestations.

You ask yourself, "if the vibrations of the current culture continue to compound in that same direction, where will we end up? Is that where we wish to be?"

If not, it is time to take action to steer the culture itself in a new direction. The feeling-tone of impending energies as a psychic imprint or intuition may also come in the form of dreams or synchronicities, to warn people and let them know that course correction is required to achieve a better outcome. The awakening ones necessarily feel a sense of responsibility to set things right, though they may meet with great resistance from the culture at large, still clinging to outworn ways of being out of fear and a misdirected desire for safety.

Course correcting may therefore seem like a monumental or even impossible feat. But knowing the foundation of the Law, there is more than hope. There is a certainty that "as a man thinketh, so is he." And as a culture thinketh, so it steers its destiny collectively.

The visionaries and changemakers are the canaries in the coal mine which warn the others it is time to shift direction. They got the vibrational memo, and their passion kicks in to assist the planetary sphere and their fellow beings with visions of new possibilities and a change of course. Utilizing the visionary power of the God Within, they tap into solutions that will bridge the gap between the faulty creations of the past and the new desired outcome ahead.

By leveraging the power of the all-knowing Source within, new dreams of harmony, sustainability and love are born to redirect sequestered consciousness into new divine designs, beneficial to all.

Since all beings are connected through Source, this energetic activism necessarily imprints the collective consciousness igniting a spark of change that eventually grows to vast proportions by seeming magic.

A seed once planted, fertilized and watered, grows into the fulfillment of the pattern it holds. This is LAW. Time and time again, this cycle of creation of civilizations and subsequent redesigns have taken place, in myriad galaxies on countless planets. It is the game and dance of Leela, the ever spinning web of phenomenal reality. Beings of Change who revel in revealing the Truth hop into planetary experiences for the sheer joy and adventure of being a Changemaker.

Endless and innumerable are the possibilities, as the hidden potential for unlimited expansion was originally planted deep within the core seed of the primary creation and Creator.

After eons of this play, the being becomes accustomed to this experience of living within the realms of manifest phenomena. And when finally, Mastery of the Laws of the Multi-verse has taken place, more joy, more fun and more love can be revealed and enjoyed.

The striving mind seeks to find ultimate solace and peace in each new creation. Ultimately, though the adventure may be grand, the adrenaline rush exhilarating and the stakes high, solace and peace will never be found there. True and lasting peace is only found within, in the full realization of the ultimate Self. There comes a time when the soul tires of the game of birthing civilizations and experiencing new life times, and yearns for HOME.

Such is the glory of this Divine Moment, that it acts as a Key Code to initiate a sequence of events that unlock the levels and layers of soul storage, to make peace within all that has been experienced. Now in the recalibrations process, any remnants of pain, suffering, blame, shame, attachment, or clinging to people, places, things, ideas and ways of being, can be discarded from the soul to lighten the load and bring clarity.

The unlocking of these Key Codes is self-regulated by the free will determination of each being. And each being is free to explore, create, and be in this creation until fully sated, and to come and go from it as it pleases.

Remember, the Essence of Source Itself IS every being. Source flung Itself in the form of sparks of light becoming myriad beings, into the phenomenal creation, for the purpose of exploration. So there is always an allowing of what is chosen by the Creator within each form. Some of you have heard the inner call and initiated this awakening sequence, experiencing new levels of insight, personal healing and awareness of the All That Is.

The first step in the journey Home is to recalibrate to this ultimate Truth in all aspects of life and living. The journey Home does not take place overnight, yet the sequence has begun, and new opportunities and fresh insights arise causing new life directions and positive decisions.

As a World Service, course corrections can be made in planetary consciousness by awakened Changemakers, to allow beings to ripen and eventually become able to fully embrace the core essence of Cosmic Principle, the knowledge and mastery of which will eventually set them free. A lifetime of service such as this is truly Service of the Highest Order.

As this Love ripens the fruit of the God Seed Within, beings grow in awareness and go to new levels of Mastery. Some call this process Ascension. The showering of this Love is like watering the tree of this God Fruit.

And so the grand stage is now set for you as Creators to emerge and shine the light and love of your long-held wisdom onto a world in need of this inspiration. Your loving service in coming to this world and activating your love and light through embracing the suffering found here acts as the in-breath of spirit, the initiation of the return HOME.

As a Creator in a world of turmoil, it is vital to harness the power and remembrance of Law, and what it means to be a Creator. You must remember how to leverage the Law in every aspect of your life with diligence as you realign yourself on all levels.

Those around you may find you strange, though they will begin to change in your midst. For your desire is strong for peace and harmony. And you have had many, many lifetimes to cultivate this desire to experience redesigning the world in your own image of Love and Harmony. The time is now to pick up the Mantle of Truth, and wear it upon your brow. As co-creators you will remember more and more, as you practice the Law.

When things seem slow in the manifestation process, it is crucial to remember that the compounded momentum in a different direction altogether has taken its toll and is still in play. Many things are being worked out and played out to completion. This is where compassion weds forgiveness, giving birth to mercy and grace. This is where mastery of the Law comes into play, for by knowing these things you shall see success.

LET US REVIEW

1. You are in essence at One with the Source itself, an emanation of this Source, God within you.

2. Compounded momentum as a result of conscious and unconscious thoughts, feelings, words and deeds have imprinted your creation and experience of reality through the Action of the Law.

3. This has occurred over eons of time.

4. The Great Law is immutable. It MUST be so to be Law, governing all. This Law has emerged as a gift of the Creator to Itself, as Creator danced forth into the unknown phenomenal reality to explore Itself. It is your rope, your tether and your anchor to the Truth and HOME.

5. Through the unconscious use of your god powers, or when you have used your powers to harm others, this Law becomes the chain that binds you to cycles of experience and suffering through compounded

momentum.

6. The course correction for god beings is to reconnect with the Source Within and comprehend the Law so that now, it can be leveraged directly, for the purposes of intentional creation.

7. The Recalibrations Process is a natural one, and is activated through a key code triggered when the soul is ready to begin the journey HOME.

8. All that which has been created and experienced in the phenomenal reality is seen and witnessed as Leela, the play of illusion. The awakened soul desires liberation, and it is liberation from being subject to the creation of its very own mind that it seeks.

9. The false gods have created traps and snares based on this Law for the purpose of sequestering the consciousness of beings. Leveraging the power of the Law in this dark way allows beings to sneakily direct that consciousness into the fulfillment of their own agendas.

10. Mercy and grace prevail as a special dispensation has

been made to liberate beings caught in such a web of self-perpetuating illusion.

11. The visionaries awaken in desire to steer the world into a new paradigm of love. They are in fact supported by the Law, as they go forth to do this, and must learn to be diligent and Master of Law in order to be successful.

12. The time is now for this Mastery Teaching to be released in your world, and the cosmos watches with baited breath as you offer that Service which will allow you to take your place among the ranks of the ascended beings of pure awareness who serve Reality, the One Truth behind all truths.

The Key Codes have been unlocked, and the stage is set for a Grand Transformation on this beautiful planet.

THE ACTION OF THE LAW: SCIENTIFIC PRINCIPLE OF THE LAW AS LORD

THE ACTION OF THE LAW is something you can depend on. During the process of awakening to it you will find that things are still clearing from the past. Do not let this worry you, only let it align you more.

It is one of the reasons for the advanced diligence protocols that are found in this teaching. The old has not yet faded away, and the new is not yet born.

It is in transition times such as this, at major galactic cyclical endings and beginnings, that help comes to the planet to assist beings in calibrating to the new energies.

This is part of a vast system of interlocking data distribution points throughout the cosmos, known as the Creator Grid. This is the signal from HOME, a neural network of God interfaced with Gaia as she enters a certain part of the cosmos.

The points of intersection between the Creator's

"homing beacon" Grid and Gaia's grid create a third grid. Many of you have felt drawn to reside on these supranodal points of the Gaia-Creator Nexus Grid.

Your energy impulses the grid and the grid impulses your energy, in a two way synchronized ongoing conversation of love. These nodal points help you access the data from this Creator Grid more readily as you prepare to spread this message of love to your planetary siblings. The time is now to awaken to the Truth of You, as a World Server on a planetary scale.

If you are reading these words, you have done this before. This is your wake up call. It is a call to take up the true role you were designed for, the role that is your divine destiny, your highest alignment with the love that you are.

As a World Server, you are poised at the edge of a planetary awakening so grand and so long awaited that the entire cosmos of awakened beings is cheering you on every moment.

The job description includes stepping fully in as a planetary steward—a visionary steward to guide the reality creation of thought forms of this planet through the conscious Operation of the Law.

As such it is a form of graduation, as an entire planet is moving to the next level of evolution in the light. Your mission, should you choose to accept, is to awaken your world through the kind act of awakening and activating yourself back to the realization of your divine origins.

As a divine being in God, you are already equipped with all the tools required to fulfill this mission.

These codes we speak of are locked within you and being revealed with each leap of consciousness you make. The OS of your being is as Secure as the Law or Lord of your life. The work you do to create harmony and beauty in your own life ripples out as vibrational waves of love, calibrating all beings around you to these higher frequencies automatically.

Higher and lower in terms of frequency, is not a judgment but a fact. A judgment would make one or more things unequivocally wrong and other things right. This fact is based on a scientific and spiritual principle of the physics (metaphysics) of life and how it operates.

A higher frequency can supersede or positively effect a lower one. As you go about your mighty work of making your day all you desire it to be, you are affecting your world in ways you have not yet realized.

The collective consciousness of a planet like earth has much residue and is in need of cleansing. The detrimental effects of the innumerable eons of unconscious creations leading into this earthly experience have caused havoc to spin out, and now, the cleanup crew is here. Your very aura itself is part of this cleansing process, automatically, which is why many if you have realized the need to take part in energy cleansing, quiet time for yourself, and meditation.

These practices are good and foundational to secure your study platform of awakening, energetic and emotional comfort, and continued well-being. Many are practicing the yogic arts, qi gong and tai chi which are also energy cleansing practices, working directly on the chakra system to dissolve old energetics that no longer serve you. Anytime you are focusing on the good stuff and that which you desire, you are necessarily impacting planetary consciousness in that direction. When the "old stuff" comes up, you can rest assured it is coming up for forgiveness, resolution and clearing.

It is possible to get stuck in the illusion during these cleansing moments, so self-care is needed to ensure you stay aligned with your highest light which will help the washing take place more gracefully. That is why it is said that as you reach for Source in your darkest moments, the highest healing and the highest service is done.

This is because that "higher power" can now come in by the sanction of your own free will choice, to rectify things in your favor. Miracles can occur, and miracles are but a reflection of the truth of God's Ever Present Love, with you, for you, as you, by you, and through you.

This Love is the unstoppable force of mercy and grace which births compassion for all created beings and all sentient life. It is through this compassion that we see clearly the folly of pushing against or making wrong that which is not desired. As keepers of the Law, we see that this great compassion birthed of love and direct personal experience, is the way to meet beings who are suffering.

We know now who *they* are, because we know who *we* are. We know where *they* have come from, because we know where *we* have come from.

We know how they got here, because we know how we got here. We know where they are going, because we know where we are going.

We came from God. We got here through the action of our impulses on the Law.

And we are going HOME—one by one, moment by moment, tear by tear, joy by joy.

THE DELETION OF KARMAS
THROUGH FORGIVENESS

REVELATION IS THE FUNCTION of the impulse of a collective to awaken. What is being revealed, but the Truth? And the Truth shall set you free, a wise being once said.

This Truth and this forgiveness have the same Source in the Law. The Lord as Law states, that which goes around comes around. So as we release others from the bondage of our own judgments, and set them free through the scientific principle of what many call forgiveness, we unleash the same freedom upon ourselves.

This dissolves the cords, ties, binds, knots, censures and punishments which we had formerly cast out to others as spells, sentencing ourselves to live by the pattern created from the words strung together in a sentence.

By casting judgment outward, we thought we were sentencing others with our words. Inasmuch as the subconscious mind of an "other" is open to receive our punishing thoughts, the damaging seed will penetrate and take root in the life of the other.

Why and how we are our brothers' and sisters' keepers now becomes crystal-clear. Would we wish damage and shame upon a precious innocent soul, if we were to finally realize the culprit and cause of all our suffering was not them, but came from within our very own selves through the Action of the Law, knowingly or unknowingly, consciously or unconsciously?

Of course we would not. Once mature enough to realize and embrace the truth of this, we become inclined to do everything in our power to rectify and dissolve any harmful energetics and their results, which we have heretofore unknowingly set into motion. The desire is for the damaging results of these unconscious actions to be dissolved for all beings impacted, through all time, space and dimension. This is a call for Total Forgiveness the Self. When we know the Truth, we immediately withdraw punishing thoughts towards self and others and make that mighty prayer we call the prayer of forgiveness.

Many have come to lose appreciation for the word forgiveness, because they get the truth that there is "nothing to forgive." They have received the teachings of the Law of Laws and realize that all is Self (the ultimate Self) and therefore Self is Cause of All.

However, the word forgiveness and the teachings behind it still have their very potent uses. It is a matter of semantics, and the invitation is to comprehend there is a deeper purpose to this revelation of what we call forgiveness, which indicates the definite internal action of "giving up of the old for the new." By giving up the old for the new, we delete the databanks of blame and shame projected onto the world that lurks within our subconscious minds, thus setting everyone and everything free from the need to suffer from our unconscious attacks any further. In this process we also set ourselves free.

This deeper teaching points to an actual experience of the truth which moves far beyond the sentimental comprehension of it.

When a being is in total realization of the working of the Law in their lives, there is a simultaneous realization of the responsibility of having previously sent out aggression, blame, hatred, criticism or cruelty through our thoughts, visualizations and feelings to other beings.

We become cognizant of the fact that our energies from past lives or those of our ancestors, may have caused harm to entire generations of beings, impregnating their receptive and innocent unconscious mind with unsavory, distorted seeds. Through understanding, instead of culpability, we can now embrace the truth of responsibility, and begin the process of cleansing and rectifying the energies we have previously and unconsciously put out through forgiveness, unconditional love, compassion, and service.

It is a beautiful moment of love when a being finally realizes this truth and acts to release all sentient beings from culpability, taking the mantle of full responsibility as the Cause of All upon the Self. Before maturity and when one still sees oneself as a lowly creature subjected to suffering, it is too terrifying to embrace this responsibility, as the fear of punishment through the action of guilt over eons is great indeed.

As a mature and ripened being, it becomes easier to "forgive and release" all others who appear to have caused harm, intentionally or unintentionally, because we realize the matrix of the way things work, and have made peace with ourselves as Cause.

The peace of forgiveness of the self is the gateway-portalway to True Divine Love. The True Divine Love of the Creator has never been apart from us, but we have held ourselves apart from it by holding ourselves culpable or guilty instead of simply "responsible."

Guilt breeds punishment as its natural course, and so of course, we have attracted eons of experiences of punishment, then wondered at the cause of it. Guilt does not allow the love of the Creator to shine through.

If we TRULY forgive ourselves as Cause, we automatically grant this forgiveness to ALL others through comprehension on a deep, authentic experiential level.

During those moments and lifetimes when we were blind to the truth, unkind remarks or criticisms of others caused more discord in the world. This gray patina of subconscious guilt remains hidden, doing its mighty work of acting upon the Law through the mechanism of our thought, word, deed and vibration, that is tinged with this guilt.

The frequencies go out and bear fruit, whether we are conscious of them or not. This has led to cycles of suffering from unknown origins, which caused beings to cry out, "Why me?" "Why are you punishing me, God?"

And it is only when the soul is strong enough to bear the truth that the nut can be cracked, the truth revealed and the message received and acted upon. We are in a time on this particular planet in which many will realize the truth and begin their journey homeward in earnest, through understanding.

THE DARK FATHER AND
THE SWORD OF JUDGMENT

THUS WE BEGIN TO SEE that all suffering has ultimately been at our own hands, and any punishment we've received has come about through the Action of the Law over much time and through many, many avenues. Beings by no means intended to curse themselves and others with so much suffering as they emerged from Source.

The Grand Experiment and its vast unknown ramifications have played out in surprising ways. The question of what would happen if we attempted to consciously separate into seeming myriad beings and give ourselves free will with a platform of unbending Law beneath it, has received its answer through our experience.

Genetic lineage imprints; imprints from this culture on this planet; imprints from past lives; energetics from the soul and spirit levels in other dimensions; and the treatment by parents of small children, have all compounded and refracted into a hall of mirrors that has been confusing at best to sort out.

The shadow self has been created when the truth of personal responsibility was judged as culpability or guilt. The impending fear of this judgment resulted in a feeling of being cut off from the Source–love, the true Self.

Nothing can possibly be more terrifying or excruciating than feeling extricated from the love that you are, which is your true existence. The experiences of this loss of love has been so traumatic, that the suppression of the guilt and fear have resulted in the growth of the darkness beyond imagining into its own seeming entity.

This entity is not real in and of itself, but it believes it is real, and it does everything it can to protect itself from getting hurt. Feeling alone, it seeks for power to satiate its anger, and for punishment to acquire some sense of control. The energy has run amok creating distortions of every kind imaginable and beyond. The black hole of desperation built here has become a seeming source unto itself, because of the power it has amassed in the subconscious. The spirit seed of beings caught in the web of this entity are as pure as every spark of light which emanated from the Creator. Yet they have over time bought into the reality of the self-created and self-perpetuating lie of separation from the One True Source, Love. And we have to remember here, that all these supposed separate beings are actually aspects of our very own Self. Herein lies the Key of Keys.

The pain and suffering endured by sentient beings because of this separation consciousness has been unimaginable. And yet it is still a testament to love as it was the longing for lost love that caused the Creator in all to go mad. The distortion has disallowed the entry of love in, and this has delayed the deep healing and cleansing necessary and desired to rectify consciousness and bring correct assessment of the situation.

This collectively created entity seeks to displace God, ironically. It has been projected as a holographic thought form birthed of deeply buried hatred and fear. The rally cry has gone out from this false god and its purveyors, to join them and take down the God whom they blame for the suffering they have experienced at their own hands. But the God which caused the suffering was their very own selves, unbeknownst to them. This is the great irony of the shadow side. The entity created is masquerading as God, yet the entity was created by God beings who forgot that they were already At One with the Source, and have God Power and God Light at their disposal to create as they desire.

They simply got caught up in the results of the unconscious operation of the Law, compounding on itself and forgetting that they were At Cause, sending themselves careening into a hole of darkness they couldn't get out of. They've projected the blame of this experience onto the Creator, falsely thinking this Creator was outside of themselves. The resultant entity gained and amassed the appearance of reality more and more with each act of darkness flung out in projection toward other beings.

Now that we have seen and begun to comprehend the mechanism of the Law here, we can only have compassion for this enormous contraction against love that we are calling the entity. Each being in the realms of this phenomenal creation has been touched by this entity in some way, and has contributed to it in some way, through unconsciousness. The Primordial Source of All stayed intact as One in "reality," and never left HOME. This Source of All desires to liberate all aspects of Itself from this delusion. Illusory though this delusion might be, experience in the phenomenal realms is very convincing and has caused the very real experience of suffering.

Because of the love of the Creator for all sentient beings, the liberation sequence has begun and is at hand in this particular plane, and all will eventually be free from the desperate madness of the false god's rampantly outpictured unconscious guilt. We are all intrinsically and necessarily by Divine Right and Divine Destiny an intricate part of the healing.

If the operation of the Law is Lord, and the dark shadow entity is attempting to take control and make itself Lord in its place, then you can see the origin of the word "outlaw." To be an outlaw in a spiritual sense is to attempt to take the Law into "one's own hands."

By forgetting the one true Law which always is, was

and will be, the entity and its collaborators have created and imposed "laws" and "rules" to "govern the minds of men." These outlaws have done a good job in some places and scenarios of seemingly eradicating the idea of the one true God. Much less do they allow the information to come out that the One True God is within each and every being, as this would give the power to the people and disallow the grand delusion to continue.

In their ignorance, those who have chosen a path of control and power over others have unconsciously cut themselves off from the healing power of personal responsibility, compassion and divine unconditional love. Instead, they seek to make slaves for the purpose of retribution from the God they believe has harmed them.

They believe God is outside of them and, and they have cast the blame for their suffering onto God erroneously, not knowing that by so doing they have condemned themselves.

The guilt that has built up within them in their subconscious minds, necessarily occurring as the result of the nature of the Action of the Law. This has caused a smoke screen that does not allow them to feel and see this Source energy within themselves which would allow them to heal. The guilt is so painful that instead it is projected out onto the world.

Entire planets have been subjugated to this torment, and the work of the Band of Mercy and the Legions of Light is seemingly eternal to restore balance and harmony in different sectors of the multi-verse. Through diligence, time, and a desire to serve the true Creator within all by liberating beings from suffering when they are ready, the work of these Legions will one day come to a close as the stage is set for the Final Act.

All beings are in conscious or unconscious preparation for this grand play, so do not feel your life and work here is for naught. You are part of a picture that is bigger and brighter than imaginable, which will one day redeem the dark father within us all, once and for all.

THE LEGIONS OF LIGHT
AND YOUR SWORD OF TRUTH

IT IS EASY TO SEE from the cosmic perspective how a polarity between legions of light and dark forces have amassed causing a seeming separation of adversaries. However, the true light holds both light and dark within it as there is nothing in creation that has come from anywhere but Source. It is difficult to understand this when you do not comprehend the nature of the Action of the Law.

Now it is time to comprehend this great Action, and how the mechanism within you operates day to day and moment to moment to mold the substance of creation itself into various manifestations.

You are ready to don the mantle of truth and pick up your sword of truth—so that you can recalibrate your entire being to the comprehension of wholeness and oneness and all that it implies.

Through this understanding, you can leverage your inner sword to cut away the falsehoods and lies of the age of separation.

Do not mistake it—this sword is a real thing—an etheric tool which you can utilize to discover the truth of a thing. By pointing the sword towards anything in your imagination and asking the Truth of it be revealed, you will access the Wisdom of the Divine Father Principle within you.

With Truth as your guide, you can continually remember that anything in creation that you're experiencing has somehow originated from a Cause you set in motion.

If it is true the Law is Lord, and you are a Creator utilizing tools of creation which are your thoughts, words, feelings and deeds, then you can know with certainty that you can easily redirect energies and set new things in motion through the intentional operation of the Law.

Thus you can with great confidence slay those thought forms and miscreations of the past that reside in the etheric planes and your subconscious mind as seeming demons and monsters, outpicturing in life as unwanted experiences and hardships.

In This way you clear the layers of detritus out of your system and attract more and more light into your field.

THE LAW IS DEPENDABLE

THE GRAND EXPERIMENT has had twists and turns that were by far unexpected, and much wisdom has been gained.

Much sadness, grief, joy, and delight have also been experienced in this realm of co-creation and all has occurred as a result of the selfsame platform of existence which was first put into place at the origins of this multi-versal experience by the prime Creator.

The Law is dependable. You can rely on this. It may take some doing to come fully into the realization of this Primary Truth, because of the effects and results of compounded momentum from eons of time, cascading into new effects and birthing new causes. But there is no effort more worthy than this that can be made by any created being.

Through understanding, you will prevail. Love shall prevail. And love shall return unto Itself, whole and complete, with much to contemplate at the end of this Grand Experiment.

But the game is not over yet!

WHO are you—and how do YOU want to play

on the Grand Stage set up before you?

The world is your oyster. And while you are all One, you are NOT alone.

Love, Father

P.S. Stop the game. Just love.

AFTERWORD: WHERE TO GO FROM HERE

This book is one part in a three-part series called Codes of Union, and is the Launching Pad of our Comprehension of the nature of Compounded Momemtnum and the Action of the Law.

Book Two, Codes of Union: Divine Mother Speaks, reveals more intricacies on the nature of energy flows, as well as further details about the Recalibrations Process mentioned herein. This book is scheduled for release in 2016.

Codes of Union Book Three, "Falling In Love with the Love Within You: Source Speaks" is also scheduled for release in late 2016. Further clarification and elucidation from the point of view of the Primordial First Cause or Principle known as the Prime Creator, God and Source will be brought to light in this tome.

Additional resources on these intrinsic teachings include "Love's Whisperings: Authentic Spiritual Development" with Chireya and The Star Elders. The Star Elders are beings dedicated to the awakening and healing of humanity who exist on multi-dimensional planes. This book provides numerous exercises and explications of the seven specific Overlays of Consciousness that have been troubling humanity, as well as layers of helpful knowledge, wisdom and material for the awakening soul.

Chireya also provides a limited number of Private Sessions as well as Online Courses, audio materials and in-person events to support the process of comprehending this leading edge material. You can discover these resources on her websites at:

Chireya.com

AnchorTheDream.com

GLOSSARY OF TERMS

The Law

The Primordial Foundation of this creational experience that says, "that which goes around comes around." The tenet "ask and you shall receive" is based on this Law. We further define "asking" as the culmination of your vibrational offering, which is the result of the utterance of your multi-dimensional being through thought, word, feeling and imagination, leading to vibrations and actions.

Action of The Law

The Action of the Law is set in motion by thoughts, words, imagination, feelings and vibrations which leads to deeds. Deeds further compound the momentum of the

Action of the Law. This Action is in continual operation, is incorruptible and is unstoppable.

Compounded Momentum

Compounded Momentum is the resultant accumulated "energy" from the operation of the Law, resulting in tendencies for further thought, word, feeling, imagination and action to go in a similar direction of the original impulse, compounded by the nature of thoughts that arise from witnessing the results as "reality" and then believing them. This is the Cause of Looping.

Looping

Compounded Momentum can cause "looping," which is also known as cycles of karma. Beings can get stuck in looping from lifetime to lifetime through the

Action of the Law resulting in compounded momentum towards a particular life pattern or patterns that seem impossible to "get out of" on one's own. Divine Intervention is sometimes in order to liberate beings from this Looping Phenomena.

Recalibrations

The process of throwing off the detritus of the ages in your mind, body, emotions and soul so that you can experience life as the original spark of Spirit, God Within You. Manifestation of your desires as Creator become much easier as you no longer carry the energetic burdens of old karmic vibrations causing cycles of unwanted repeated patterns (looping). You may contact Chireya at Chireya.com if you would like to learn about, train in or work with her in the Recalibrations Process.

God Within You

God Within You is the truth of you—the prime, original essence of pure Divine Love—the Source from which you came, to which you will return, and the Essence of Which you Are.

The Self

Another word for the God Within You empowered by many sages such as Ramana Maharishi, Yogananda and many others. Jesus said, "The Kingdom of Heaven is Within You."

Source

The effulgent, effervescent, overflowing, all-knowing, all-seeing, all-feeling, all powerful Essence of Life Itself. The Creator of All Creators. The Fountainhead of All Life.

The Grand Experiment

Father explains this particular experience of Creation as a Grand Experiment which "we" as aspects of Source willingly embarked upon, to discover more about ourselves through a Cosmic Adventure of formerly unheard of proportions.

Truth vs. "truth"

The word "truth" is controversial in the worldly sense. There are many who would argue there is no ultimate truth. Semantically speaking, Truth with a capital "T" in this book refers to the Source Creator as the ultimate Self of your very own Being, and the Law as the impersonal Lord of this Creation. Thus it is the foundational Truth upon which all of creation is built and from which all of creation springs.

Spelled with a lower case "t," truth refers to those "truths" which different people and cultures and civilizations have created or adopted over time through their observation of "reality."

Father (Divine Father)

Divine Father or First Father is the masculine aspect of the Source of All known as God or Prime Cause. The first of two emanations from Prime Cause, at the beginning of this phenomenal Creation, are called Divine Mother and Divine Father in these works.

Coupled with Divine Mother, this Divine Father aspect completes the circuitry of love that becomes the generative engine or "energy" that drives creation forward. He holds the Mantle of Self Responsibility & Discernment, and offers the Gift of the Sword of Truth.

Divine Mother

Divine Mother or First Mother as spoken of in

these writings represents the Feminine aspect of Source, God, Prime Cause. She is the equal part of the Primary Dual Emanation from Source or Prime Cause with Divine Father or First Father. Together with Her Twin Flame Divine Father, she is the required matching component of the generative engine of all creation.

She holds the Mantle of Eternal Love Without Conditions and the Full and Total Remembrance of Our Innate, Intrinsic Innocence, which is the counter-balance and compliment to Divine Father's Sword of Truth and Tenet of Self Responsibility. They are two sides of one coin.

Also Known as PATER & MATER

Comprehending that these Essences of Masculine and Feminine are within All is known as the Heiros Gamos, or Divine Marriage.

Pater and Mater are the Essences of Divine Father and Divine Mother in Creation, understood as the seed and the soil, the sperm and the ovum, the pattern and matter. The Matrix of Light Filaments of the original divine Matrix or "Mother" gives berth / birth to the formative structure / blueprint of the "Father" such that He can Go Forth and Experience Creation. She "holds" him — and all of us — in her Sea of Eternal Grace and Love.

She therefore "pre-exists" Him and "allows" Him to "express" in this Grand Experiment. Keep in mind that the masculine and feminine essences herein explained are "a way" of describing a culmination of creation based on our current easiest comprehension and perceptual abilities at the current time and in our current framework.

Mater and Pater are thus explained as, the Formative and Causative Impulses of Phenomenal Reality, creating an "engine" which flows electrical light impulses through the filaments of Light throughout the Multi-verse to birth and sustain it.

Said another way, they are the First Emanations of Source, which together united through a spiraling caused by their differentiation, are indelibly intertwined and birthed all Created Beings and initiated Creation as instruments of Prime Cause-Source in this Grand Experiment.

Infinity

Infinity is herein understood as representing the never ending, looping cycles of phenomenal existence.

Eternity

Eternity is herein reflected upon as the nature of immortality and endless life beyond the flesh and entirely beyond the phenomenal reality, based in our true HOME as Source. Eternity is always accessible from within our quantitative experience of Infinity.

Sword of Truth

The Sword of Truth is a Gift of Divine Father, utilized as a tool to discover the truth of a thing; to cut away that which is no longer needed in life; to decide and "make decisions" by cutting to the chase of what is truly the best choice in any moment; and to align with the masculine generative power for the purpose of true and lasting healing.

Cup of Innocence

The Shield of Innocence is the Armament of the Divine Mother, and can be utilized as a tool to remember your eternal nature as an Innocent Child of God and Life; to melt away the pain of suffering in a pool of unconditional love; and to calibrate your soul to the original Divine Spark of your true spiritual essence, which emanated directly from Source / First Mother / First Father at the beginning of this phenomenal existence.

Forgiveness

Forgiveness is The Master Key to recalibrating your life through the unconditional awareness of Truth. Forgiveness is "giving up of the old data and beleifs" for the new and eternal Truth of yourself as one with Cause. A wise man once said, "Ye are Gods."

ABOUT CHIREYA

CHIREYA ARIGURUDEVI is a scribe and orator for the lineages of light, in service to Source as a conduit for codes, information and energy which ignites the spark of Pure Spirit within beings for the purpose of awakening to the Truth of our Cosmic Heritage as Beings of God and divine co-creators.

For more information and to contact Chireya about her Light Transmissions Energetic Alignment Sessions, Life Architecture Coaching or other matters, please visit Chireya.com.

www.ingramcontent.com/pod-product-compliance
Lightning Source LLC
LaVergne TN
LVHW041224080426
835508LV00011B/1074